15035 EN
Living in a World with AIDS

Forbes, Anna
B.L.: 4.5
Points: 0.5   MG

The AIDS Awareness Library™

Living in a World with AIDS

Anna Forbes, MSS

The Rosen Publishing Group's
PowerKids Press™
New York

Published in 1996 by The Rosen Publishing Group, Inc.
29 East 21st Street, New York, NY 10010

First Edition

Book design: Erin McKenna

Photo credits: Cover by Sarah Friedman; p. 7 © Mark Bolster/International Stock; p. 12 © Robert Burke/Liaison International; p. 20 © Michael Philip Manheim/International Stock; all other photos by Guillermina DeFerrari.

Forbes, Anna, MSS.
    Living in a world with AIDS / Anna Forbes.
       p.   cm.— (The AIDS awareness library)
    Includes index.
    Summary: Introduces readers to AIDS, the disease caused by HIV viruses, tells how people become infected and how to avoid infection.
    ISBN 0-8239-2367-3 (hardcover)
    1. AIDS (Disease)—Juvenile literature. [1. AIDS (Disease) 2. HIV infections. 3. Diseases.] I. Title. II. Series.
RC607.A26F627 1996
616.97'92—dc20   96-5531
                                                          CIP
                                                          AC

Manufactured in the United States of America

Contents

A Disease Called AIDS

This is a book about a disease called AIDS. Over 500,000 people in the United States have AIDS. About one million people have HIV, the **virus** (VY-rus) that can cause AIDS.

Thinking about AIDS is sad or scary for lots of people. Some people don't like to talk about it. These people may not understand that the more you know about something, the less scary it is. This book tells you how people get HIV and AIDS. It also tells you how you can stay safe from HIV and AIDS.

◀ Your mom may be one person you can ask for the facts about HIV and AIDS.

What Is HIV?

HIV is the virus that can cause AIDS. Viruses cause many different diseases. For example, colds and chicken pox are both started by viruses. But HIV is different from any other virus in two main ways.

- People have HIV for a long time before they get sick with AIDS.
- HIV is very hard to pass from one person to another.

Someone with HIV can do many of the things that someone without HIV can do. ▶

Getting Sick with AIDS

HIV takes a long time to make a person sick. The virus that causes chicken pox makes a person sick in about two weeks. A cold virus can give a person a cold within a day or two. But people with HIV don't get sick with AIDS for about ten years. In fact, a person with HIV may look and feel healthy. She may get AIDS when her body is tired and worn out from fighting HIV. But this can take many years.

◀ You can't tell if someone has HIV or AIDS just by looking at him or her.

How Do People Get HIV?

HIV lives in human blood. It also lives in the body fluids that adults' bodies make for having sex. For HIV to travel, it has to go from one person's body right into another person's body. It mostly travels from one person to another when two people have sex in an unsafe way or share needles to use drugs together.

You can't get HIV from being coughed on, sneezed on, or kissed by someone who has HIV or AIDS. You can't get HIV just by living with or visiting someone with HIV or AIDS.

You can't get HIV or AIDS by spending time with someone who has it. ▶

Knowing If You Have HIV

People have their blood tested to find out if they have HIV. When people have HIV but are not sick, we say they are **HIV-positive** (HIV POZ-ih-tiv). This means that they have the virus that can cause AIDS, but they don't have AIDS. Some people have been HIV-positive for as long as fifteen years without getting AIDS.

Kids and HIV

Almost everyone with HIV got it from having sex or by sharing needles to use drugs. Since most kids don't have sex or use drugs, most kids don't get HIV. If you use drugs, stop right away. Talk to a teacher, your parents, or another adult about how to stop and how to say no to friends who push you to try drugs. If someone is making you have sex with them, tell an adult right away. This isn't a secret you should keep. No one has the right to make you do something that hurts you. And having sex right now can hurt you.

Talk to an adult about how to say no to people who offer you drugs. ▶

How Do Kids Get HIV?

The only way you and most kids can get HIV is if you have a fresh cut or scratch on your skin and someone else's blood gets into it. That person would have to have HIV or AIDS for you to get HIV. Unbroken skin is a good **shield** (SHEELD) against HIV. Never cut or scratch yourself on purpose. Sometimes kids want to become "blood brothers" or "blood sisters." They each cut themselves, then rub the cuts together, promising to be friends forever. Friends are great. But you don't need to make blood promises!

◀ Shaking hands or giving a high five
is a great way to seal a friendship.

17

Helping Safely

You can't tell by looking if someone has HIV or not. So be careful whenever you help someone else. If you see someone who is bleeding, find an adult who can help him or her. If there are no adults around, yell "help" as loudly as you can. Keep yelling until someone comes.

While you're waiting for help, give the person who is bleeding a towel, tissues, a coat, a shirt, or any piece of cloth to press on the cut. Pressing down on a cut will help it stop bleeding. By having the person who is hurt press on the cut, you can help and still stay safe.

Never touch someone else's blood. ▶

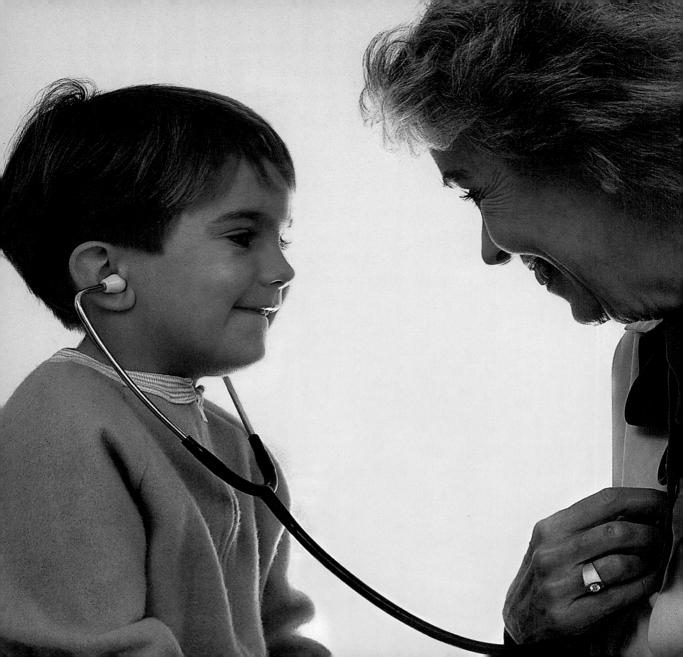

AIDS from the Doctor?

Doctors, nurses, and dentists wear **plastic** (PLAS-tik) gloves to protect themselves from HIV. Even people who make **tattoos** (tat-TOOZ) or pierce people's ears wear gloves.

Doctors and nurses also use **sterile** (STAYR-ul) needles for giving shots. Sterile means super clean. You can't get HIV or any other disease from a sterile needle. So going to the doctor or dentist is safe. You don't have to worry about getting HIV there.

◀ You can't get HIV or AIDS from your doctor. But you can talk to her about HIV and AIDS.

Who Has HIV or AIDS?

You can't tell by looking whether a person has HIV or AIDS. He or she may not look or feel or act sick. So how do you stay safe from getting HIV or AIDS? In the same ways we talked about before. Don't touch someone else's blood. And don't have sex or use drugs, especially drugs that use needles.

If you practice HIV and AIDS safety, you can keep yourself safe no matter who you're with.

Glossary

HIV-positive (HIV POZ-ih-tiv) Having HIV.
plastic (PLAS-tik) Human-made, flexible, nonmetal material.
shield (SHEELD) Something that gives protection.
sterile (STAYR-ul) Very clean.
tattoo (tat-TOO) Design made with ink injected into skin.
virus (VY-rus) Germ that causes disease.

Index

CUENTO
DE LUZ

For Zaira, who's got it all: a pretty name, a big heart,
and now, a story dedicated to her.

*May children dream
like birds in flight.*

Zaira and the Dolphins

Text © 2011 Mar Pavon
Illustrations © 2011 Cha coco
This edition © 2011 Cuento de Luz SL
Calle Claveles 10 | Urb Monteclaro | Pozuelo de Alarcón | 28223 Madrid | Spain | www.cuentodeluz.com
Original title in Spanish: Zaira y los Delfines
English translation by Jon Brokenbrow

ISBN: 978-84-15241-65-2

Printed by Shanghai Chenxi Printing Co., Ltd. in PRC, July 2011, print number 1216-07

FSC
www.fsc.org
MIX
Paper from
responsible sources
FSC® C007923

Zaira
and the
Dolphins

Mar Pavon

Illustrated by Cha Coco

Just like she did every day, Zaira went to the
fountain in the square to see the dolphins.
She went with Spooky, her best friend.

"Look! The dolphins are playing! They're balancing balls on their noses!" gasped Zaira, absolutely thrilled.

Spooky smiled too, but all of the children who were in the square looked at them with strange expressions on their faces.

"Who are you talking to? What do you mean, the dolphins are playing? There's nothing in the fountain except water. And water doesn't play!"

Zaira and Spooky weren't listening. They were too busy watching the dolphins!

The next day after school, Zaira returned to her favorite place: the fountain in the square. This time, her boyfriend Indigo went with her.

"Look, Indigo!" she shouted with glee. "Today the dolphins are jumping as high as the water from the spout!"

Indigo admitted that it was a really amazing feat, but the children playing in the square looked on with puzzled expressions on their faces.

"Who's Indigo? And what dolphins are jumping? There's nothing in this fountain except water! And water doesn't jump!"

Instead of listening to them, Zaira and Indigo watched the dolphins and sat on the edge of the fountain with their arms around each other, just the way that boyfriends and girlfriends do.

Another afternoon, Zaira convinced her twin sister Gemma to come along with her to watch the dolphins.

"Can you hear the dolphins, Gemma? Today they're singing songs!"

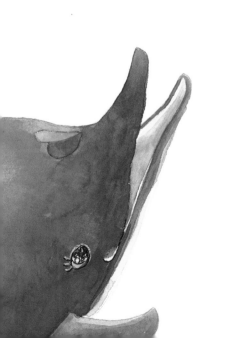

Gemma clapped happily.
But the children who were playing around them didn't understand anything.

"Who's Gemma? And where can you see dolphins singing songs? There's nothing in this fountain except water. And water sounds like water!"

Zaira and Gemma didn't hear them—all they wanted to listen to were the dolphins!

But one day, Zaira discovered that the fountain was empty. Some of the children, seeing the surprise on her face, made fun of her.

"Oh, what a pity! Dolphin Girl's run out of water!"
"And she's run out of dolphins!"
"What's the crazy little girl going to do now?
Maybe she'll go looking for whales in a puddle!"

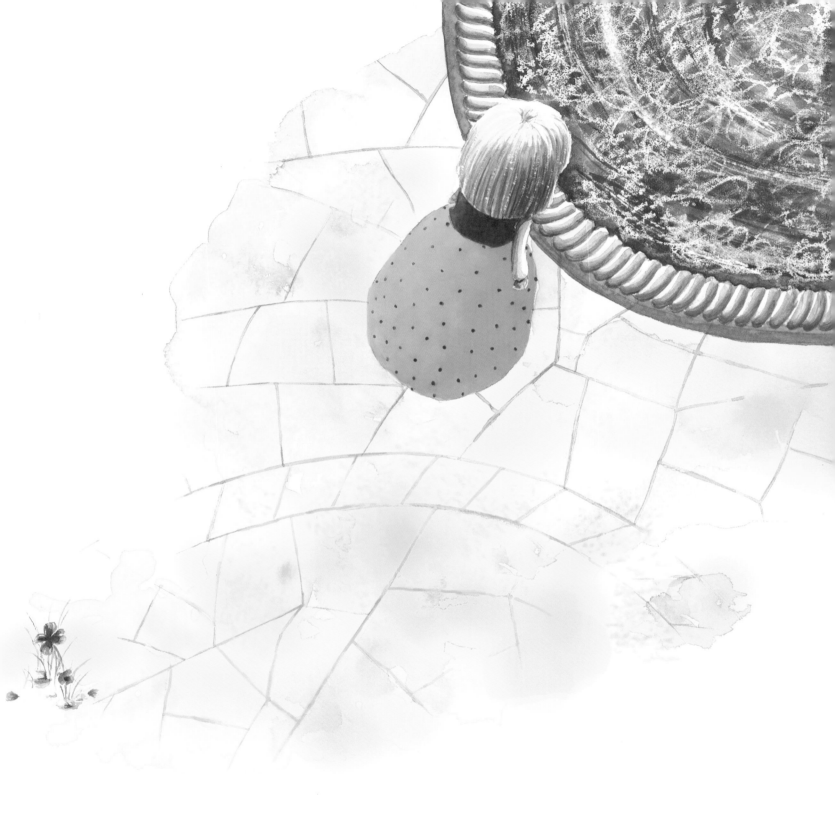

All of the children who played in
the square were laughing and jeering.
But Zaira was about to burst into tears.

And then, all of a sudden, the fairy
Takethat appeared in front of her,
right in the middle of the fountain!

The first thing Takethat did was wipe the smiles off the faces of the children who were laughing at Zaira.

"Take that!" she said, proud of what she'd done.

At the same time, Zaira began to smile. Then the fairy asked her:
"Would you like to see some whales in a puddle?"

Unsure, Zaira said,
"Yes…well, no… well, I don't know…"

But her smile turned to laughter when
Takethat asked her:
"Would you rather see your beautiful dolphins?"

"Oh yes!" said Zaira, "more than anything in the
world!"

"Alright, then. The only thing you have to do is
go home, behave yourself, and watch closely
what's going on around you!"

Zaira obediently did everything Takethat had told her: she returned home, she behaved better than ever, and of course, she kept her eyes wide open all evening.

But the dolphins didn't appear. Zaira looked for them in the washbasin, in the toilet, in the watering can, in the kitchen sink, in a glass of water, and even in the mop bucket! But she couldn't find any sign of them.

Finally, it was bath time, something Zaira had hated since she was a baby. But despite her protests, her Mom insisted on bathing her every day, and that evening was no exception.

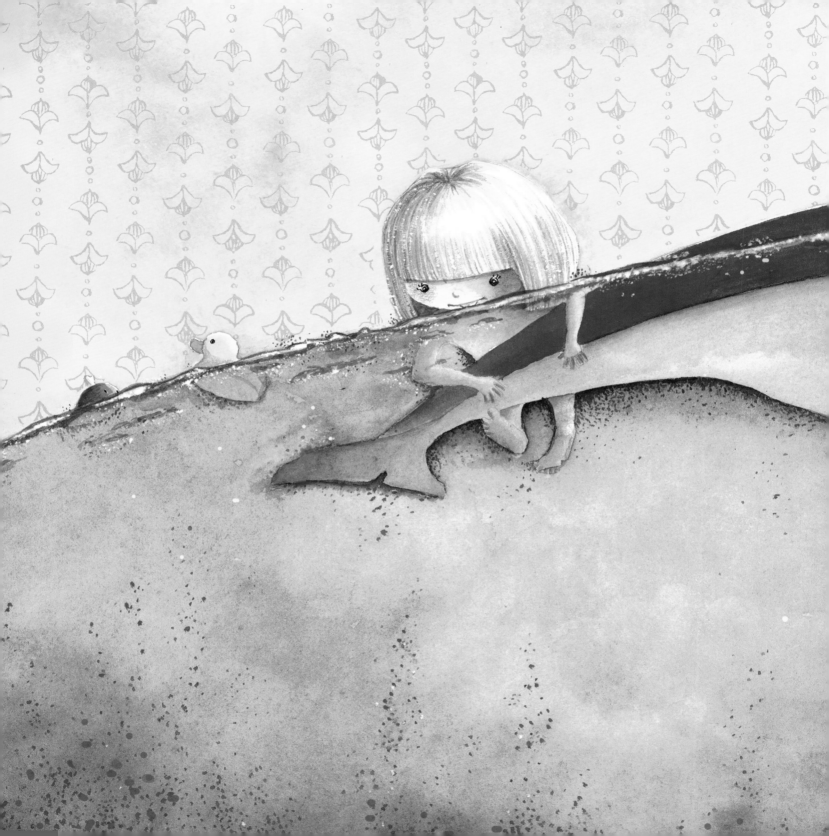

Suddenly, Zaira felt something bumping against her.
There were two of them, and they were tickling her
tummy so much that she couldn't stop giggling.

"Goodness me,
Zaira, I've never seen
you enjoy bath time
so much!" said Mom
with surprise.

Finally, the dolphins let her come up for air. Zaira made the most of the opportunity, and shouted:

"Spooky! Indigo! Gemma! Come and see the dolphins! They're here with me in the bath, and they're tickling me!"

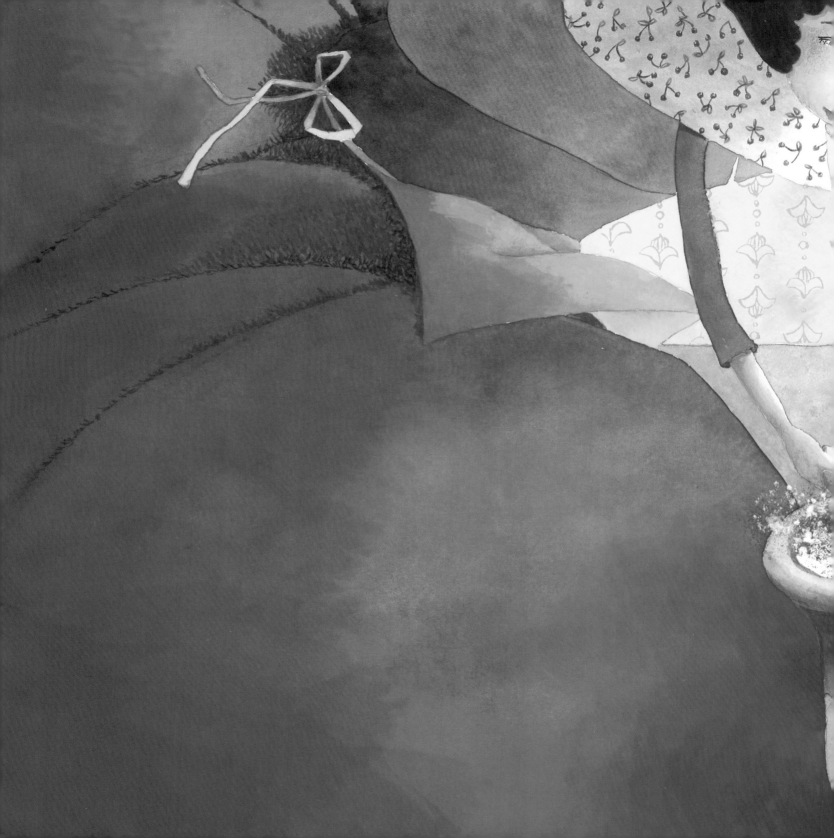

"I didn't know there were so many of us in this house!" laughed Mom, as she tried to wash Zaira.

But Zaira was too busy splashing around and giggling.

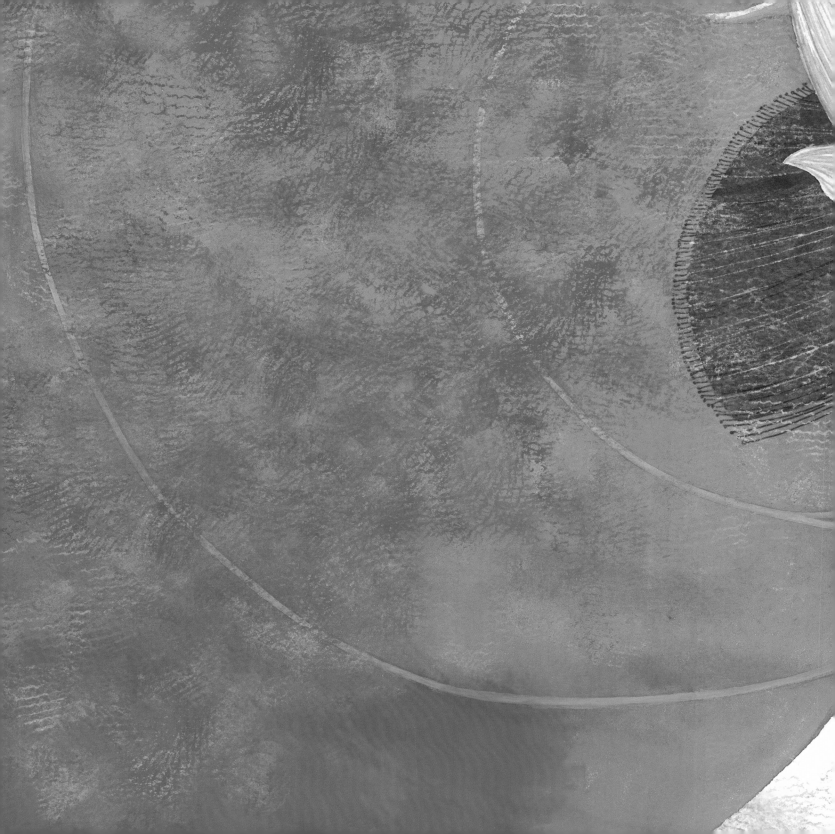

And just then, a certain fairy took the opportunity to wipe the steam off the mirror with her wand, see her reflection, and, with a wink in her eye, say in a very satisfied voice:

"Take that!"